Whiskey Breath
Poetry

Kirk Ferguson

Presentation by *BookLeaf Publishing*

Web: www.bookleafpub.com

E-mail: info@bookleafpub.com

ISBN: 9789357696401

First edition 2023

The Spastic Scholastic

I'm the Spastic Scholastic
Always fantastic
Words appear like magic
Never tragic

So be a man
Take a stand
Snap right back like a rubber band

Take my hand
We'll go explore
Down and up the walls
Ceiling to the floor

Take my thoughts
Twisted them up
Pop a top and fill my cup

Tip it up
Drink it down
Look at me go
I'm flying now

Soar up high
Watch the lights below
Tongue not tied
Spit a spastic flow

Feeling courageous
Words can be dangerous
Sting more then a fist
A welt on your skin
With the flick of the wrist

Tongue like elastic
Dick never flaccid
Spit like I'm rabid
Burn ya like acid
Flow like the river
Make your legs quiver
Give ya a shiver
Like the wind when it blows

A bag of weed
A friend I need
Roll it up like tumbleweed
Take a hit then pass to me

We're cooking baby
Cooking with fire
Or was it grease
Infecting your eardrums
Like a spreading disease

Open them up and listen to me
Feel the rhythm
From your head to your feet
Tap your foot and feel the beat

Smile

Let the light shine through
Keep your head up high
Give negativity the boot
And keep your eyes on the prize

Be proud of yourself
Don't let anyone get you down
we can can love one another
and turn this world around

Hatred, greed and evil folks
The world has just to many
I say again this isnt a joke
Not even remotely funny

Always wear a smile
It looks so amazing you see
When you have a positive attitude
It flows from you to me

Wether it be Negative or positive
Our attitudes are always contagious
With all the hate in the world
Things really are getting quite dangerous

More division in the world
Then one should ever see
I don't feel I'm better then you
Do you think your better then me?

Poisonous words make us sick
Some folks choose these words swiftly
Stop criticizing one another
And spread some positivity

The power of a smile is amazing
It can simply change ones day
Even when times are tough
It can help us find the way

So always keep your head up
stay bright in the darkest days.
Every storm will pass
when the wind blows the clouds away.

Suspect

It was a bright sunny day
In the middle of the night
There was a terrible accident
It gave us an awful fright
Upon investigation
The details were hard to get right
The blind man said he seen it
Even though he has no sight
To make it even stranger
Things getting extremely weird
The deaf man said he heard it
Although he can not hear
Getting nowhere fast
The details surely doomed
The next move was to ask
The bravest man within the room
We figured maybe he would be
The one to set things straight
But when the accident happen
He simply died of fright
Then we turned our heads
To the biggest coward inside the place
Chest puffed out
Showing off his might
Confidence upon his face
Blind man said he seen it coming
Deaf man heard something run away
Details are still pretty foggy

But the mute man had lots to say
Nothing of any importance
Just honestly surprised to hear him talk
Then the crippled man in the wheelchair
Jumped up and began to walk
Not a clue where he was going
But it appeared as though he was done
He opened up the door
Took off in a run
And now My only question.....
Was he the guilty one?

Bones in the Closet

There are dusty old bones.
Hidden inside.
Waiting for their moment.
To come out from hiding.

There's skeletons in my closet.
We pick each others bones.
They only come out to play.
When no one else is home.

The brittle bones pure evil.
Not hidden very well.
Peeking through the key hole.
From the firey pits of hell.

Boney fingers reach out.
Beckoning for my hand.
I try to pull away.
But my attention they demand.

Their bones are always rattling.
Just behind the door.
I hope they don't go tattling.
Spit a bone out on the floor.

Choking on the remnants.
Of a long lost memory.
Hell will gain a tenant.
When they take the life from me.

I cant turn back the hour glass
And turn glass back into sand
Buy I can accept my destiny
And take it like a man

Ghost Lantern

The night was dark and the feeling dreary.
The chill down my spine felt oh so eeri.
I felt a presence, like I wasn't alone.
Was i not by myself?
Was I not on my own?

What was it exactly that I seen through the trees?
The feeling that something stared back at me.
A knot in my stomach soon began to twist.
Was there something else out there?
Did it really exist?

Was it Jesus Christ or a Poltergeist?
A figment of my imagination?
What the hell was I was dealing with?
Some sort of an abomination?

A Lone Ghost Lantern hung in the air.
Almost as if something was holding it there.
Was it trying to tell me, "I better beware."
Whatever it was it gave me a scare.

It moved as though one, would think it was carried.
Heart beating fast, extremely worried.
I froze for a moment with nowhere to go.
The silence was deafening, as it moved too and fro.

Trying not to lose my mind, I slowly backed away.
Exactly what that presence was, one could not say to this very day.
Soon the wind picked up and the trees began to sway.
I am not a religious man but that day I began to pray.

Running for my cabin, my legs kept moving faster.
While all through the forest, roaored a murderous laughter.
To scared to look behind, I finally reached my shelter.
I closed the door behind me, to protect me from this helter skelter.

Safe inside my cabin, or at least that's what I hoped.
Surrounded by a familiar place seemed to help me cope.
Sitting upon the table was a lantern of my own.
Maybe once I light it, I wouldn't feel so all alone.

I lit the Wick and soon, the flame began to Shimmer.
But only for a moment, did my hope begin to Glimmer.
The door began to shake and the windows fiercely rattled.
I pushed a chair against the door and hoped the windows wouldn't shatter.

The breeze that crept over my skin, one could call it haunting.
Once thought to be safe inside, its presence seemed now to taunt me.

There was an Odour now that filled the room
something old, musty and rotten.
Was this some sort of tormented soul, once lost and
soon forgotten?

Death was knocking at my door and I wouldn't let it
in.
I was scared half to death but just couldn't let it win.

That Lone Ghost Lantern all alone, hovering in the
wind.

No longer could I resist, it was time to face my fears.
There's no more use in hiding, it already knows I'm
here.
Of all the fears I've faced, this one was the darkest.
I was very unsure the outcome since we are being
honest.

I knew it was wrong as I ripped open the door.
Puffed up my chest and let out a roar.
"You will not defeat me, don't you even try."
"I will not bow down to you."
"I will never comply."

For a moment the wind continued then slowly began
to die.
Was this hellish moment over between this thing and
I?
So Close i could have touched it, Suspended in front
of me.

The Lone Ghost Lantern flickered gently, almost
seeming pleased.

Now the wind had all died down and the howling had
all stopped.
It was so silent inside the house, you could hear a
lone pin drop.
Reaching out my hand to see if it was real.
Was it my imagination? It was all just so surreal.

As slowly as it had approached, it began to fade
away.
And it was never seen again, since that fateful day.
The Lone Ghost Lantern, faded into the night.
I watched it from my doorway as the night absorbed
the light.

Battle Scars

I have no legacy to leave.
No massive fortune to spend.
No royal chariots are awaiting.
For my arrival in the end.

I'm no knight in shining Armour.
My Armour, tarnished and worn.
Covered, with dents and rust.
I'm no rose, but instead the thorn.

My Lance, is bent and broken.
No longer do I charge ahead.
Instead of running into battle.
I take the high road instead.

My shine has all but faded.
I no longer see the light.
Sometimes I wonder why I'm here.
Battling wrong and right.

Theres promise on the horizon.
Hope of better days.
Woke up on the right side of life.
And blood, still pumps through my veins.

The battered shield I carry.
Keeps it all concealed.
My army marches forward.
With the defenses that I wield.

Battle scars cover my skin.
Another wound with a story to tell.
But there's still a beating heart.
Inside this broken Shell.

Liquored with Lucifer

I was sitting in a dingy old bar on the wrong side of
the tracks.
The kind of place where the degenerates seemed to
fall between the cracks.

A place where ones back was safer against a wall.
Some colorful characters amongst the crowd keeping
me enthralled.

The dusty old jukebox in the corner played some
depressing country song.
A cloud of smoke hovered the room and the smell of
stale booze was strong.

No such thing as happy hour when you drink in a
place like this.
Not only did it smell of stale booze but it also reeked
of piss.

The whiskey burned my throat as I downed a couple
of shots.
Suddenly, I was overcome by a smell as if something
had started to rot.

I noticed a reflection of someone behind me in the
mirror behind the bar.
Spinning around on my stool the first thing I noticed
were his facial scars.

The burning embers of a lit cigarette cast a pale light
on the man's features.
With every puff he took the lines on his face became
a little clearer.

Ashes fell from the tip as they grew to long and
heavy to stay attached.
Drawing my eye to the knife on his belt that looked
all beat up and scratched.
My attention and curiosity he surely did attract.

Ashes cascaded gently to the ground as I stared in
awe at this mysterious man.
The tips of his fingers turning yellow from the
cigarette in his hand.

He wore a wide brimmed hat all tattered, torn and
black.
His long dark stringy hair hung down the middle of
his back.

He pulled down his hat as if to hide his hollow
sunken eyes.
He appeared to only be a shell of a man, a creature of
his own demise.

The smell of burnt flesh flared my nostrils as his
cigarette burned to a nub.
The smoke from his fingers burned my eyes so I gave
them both a rub.

His breathe smelled of cheap whiskey and he wore a
long beat up leather coat.
Was this man before me a dealer of death, determined
and fully devote.

He didn't appear to be a mortal man and I wondered
if I was looking at a ghost.
My heart thumped loudly in my ears as I tried to
swallow the lump in my throat.

His dirty, weathered skin looked like worn out leather
hide.
The hat he wore atop his head adorned with a single
black feather on the side.

Who the hell was this man and why was he standing
there staring at me?
Was this man who stood before me cursed or was he
holier then thee?

"Grab yourself a drink my friend, now come pull up a
stool."
Every person in the bar heard the tension in my voice
as I tried to play it cool.

"Two whiskeys for me and my partner here, just to be
safe better make them doubles."
"Have a drink on me."
"I just want it to be known I don't want any trouble."

His threatening figure drew even closer as he sat on
the stool beside me.

He had yet to utter a single word as he sat down on
his seat so silently.

The stench of death almost overwhelming as it oozed
from all his pores.
By the Haggered look upon his face he'd been
through many wars.

He looked at me with wild eyes, he seemed not to be
stable
"The only way to save your soul is to drink me under
the table."

The bartender set two doubles in front of us on the
sticky counter top.
He drank them both himself then motioned the
bartender to fill them up.

The barkeep poured two more doubles, and the man
pushed them in my direction.
Stepping up to the plate I shot my 90 proof injection.

Again he beckoned the bartender to fill them both
back up.
The barkeep could barely keep his hands from
shaking as he topped up the filthy cups.

You could feel the tension in the room, heavy like a
weight.
Double after double, how long could I go if we kept
on pounding them straight.

My eyes were getting blurry and my legs they felt
like rubber.
Every shot I choked down made my insides shudder.

Drink for drink, a competition taking place for my
soul.
"If you don't want an eternity in hell," he said, you
will do just as you were told.

"Any type of liquor, name your poison son."
Already in the midst of battle, I pointed to the bottle
of rum.

Hammering back the drinks, matching one another
ounce for ounce.
We battled long into the night with our alcoholic
joust.

Another shot of rum, whiskey and vodka too.
Bottle after bottle, we continued to push on through.

He showed no signs of stopping and he wasn't
backing down.
I was swimming in so much liquor that night, I'm
surprised I didn't drown.

The last couple of shots he choked down as he
swallowed extremely hard.
Three sheets to the wind, I slammed two more with
complete and utter disregard.

The more I drank the less I cared and felt as if I
sobered a little.
The dirty jukebox now blaring a song with some
upbeat country fiddle.

The son of a bitch swayed back and forth almost
falling off his stool.
My adrenaline pumped and I felt as though I was
drinking rocket fuel.

Quitting isn't an option when you drink against the
dead.
Thoughts of life and immortality spiraling in my
head.

It was then the bartender spoke up and slowly began
to speak.
Reaching under the bar he picked up a bottle that
looked antique.

"I have something here that will send a chill down the
center of your spine."
Blowing the dust off the bottle, he spun the top off
his finest homemade shine

He filled two foggy glasses and set them before us on
the bar.
My ears now soaking up the sound of some twangy
country guitar.

I wished I hadn't smelled it first, the stench burned
into my sinuses.

Two feet, I jumped right in but wasn't making any
Promises.

The moment it hit my lips I knew the choice I made
was wrong.
Every muscle in my body tightened, this liquor was
just to strong.

Trying to focus my watering eyes and keep this
demon down.
We had already drank the bar near dry and it was long
since I lost count.

There was a burning in my stomach and it moved up
to my throat.
But I refused to give up, even if I choked.

Ordering the barkeep to "keep em coming," he lined
us up two more.
It wouldn't be too long now before one of us hit the
floor.

My nemesis now hunched over the bar trying
desperately to balance himself.
In order to save my soul that night I had to drink
every drop on the shelf.

I'd either save my soul or drink myself to death so the
bastard couldn't win.
We must have been at least, four or five sheets into
the wind.

He didn't seem so scary now with shoulders hunched
and head hung down.
And my condition was not much better then his as I
ordered another round.

He wobbled and he weaved and soon his chest
heaved.
Then he threw up a big pile of bones.

The windows and the doors blew open forcefully
with a gust.
Then him and his bones simply turned into dust.

They swirled in the wind as it whipped through the
bar.
What the hell was happening this was all so bizarre.

As fast as it came it was gone just as soon.
The look of shock and surprise on every face in the
room.

In my liquor fueled haze, wondering if I
hallucinated.
Was I truly this close to my soul being completely
decimated?

That was the night I drank against the dead and came
close to meeting my maker.
 Death came knocking but I didn't answer, not tonight
Mr. Undertaker.

Are you awake

He lay in bed beside her
Silently watching her sleep
Only a few hours ago
His love was buried deep

Exhausted from the passion
Deep into her slumber
Putting his hand on her back
He gently began to rub her

Starting at her shoulders
Smooth skin under his hand
Moving up to her hair
Sliding his fingers between the strands

She began to stir a little
And let out a little sigh
His hand now moving lower
Massaging her buttocks and thighs

Stirring from her sleep
'Psst, are you awake?'
I hope you've enjoyed your nap
We have more love to make.

Tonight is yours

Lay back my dear and close your eyes
I have something for you, a little surprise

My hands take your feet and gently rub
Hot water is currently filling the tub

I want you to know
I'm happy your mine
Open your eyes
I've poured you some wine

Lay back, relax and enjoy your drink
You've been working so hard
You need "me time" I think

Strong and determined you work hard everyday
Always so busy with little time to play

No need to fight it you just need some rest
I'll continue my massage to help you destress

I've lit some candles for your time in the bath
My hands working magic like an osteopath

The tightness and knots release from your body
My hands make you perkier then any cup of coffee

Now enjoy your bath my darling
Your wine and candle light
Take all the time you need
Because tonight is, your night

The Insanity of my Profanity

I want my Goals to be attainable
But some resources are Unavailable
My Visions are Untamable
Sometimes my mind unstable
I often wonder if I'm capable
Guaranteed I'm willing and able
Shall I be honest or create a fable
Work everyday to keep bread on the table
Children quickly outgrow their cradles
I have no horses in my stable
But keep soup within the ladel
No need to play me a fiddle
Life can be like a riddle
Sometimes we double dribble
We often stumble a little
Our bones sometime feel brittle
Sometimes we feel commital
The Insanity of my Profanity
Underneath this fleshy Canopy
Mind packed with thoughts of Depravity
Consumed with my own mortality
I struggle to face reality
Pushing forward with all my audacity
Dreams of defying gravity
Take me to a world of fantasy
Will I bask in my own vanity
Or in actuality
Struggle with my own morality

Halloween

There's a Blood red moon on the rise.
All the faces around you disguised.
The daylight finally demised.
As the Shadows bring on the night.

The Swaying tress make Shadows dance.
While Zombies walk, the streets entranced.
All the Ghosts and ghouls begin to appear.
While some folks tremble with horror and fear.

From the carved face of a jack o lantern.
Flickers a dim candle light.
Awaiting the ghouls to make their return.
Under the moon thats shining bright.

Off in the distance a Werewolf growls.
A chilling wind begins to howl.
Decorations of Orange and brown.
Haunting spirits patrol the town.

Can't control the feelings of impending doom.
The haunting glow of the Blood red moon.
Silhouette of a witch across it zooms.
A night light for all the Ghastly ghouls.
Hoping for daylight to come again soon.

Will you be playing tricks or eating treats.
While the demons March up and down your streets.
Scary Ghosts look like floating sheets.
In a dark alley I would not want to meet.

Costumes help keep our identities unseen.
Each and every Halloween.
From Angels to Devils and all in between.
The purely innocent.
The grotesquely obscene.

Anything you could imagine.
In your wildest dreams.

Time

The clock on the wall, makes no sound at all.
The tick has lost its tock.

Time slips away always ours to waste.
Our existence on the chopping block.

We count the minutes and days as our years
become numbered.
When any second we could cease to exist.

If you could do anything in your wildest dreams.
What would you write on your list?

Would you push yourself to be a better you?

Challenge yourself to conquer your fears?

Never give up and work your ass off?

Push forward through the sweat and tears?

Be the best you and truly exel.
You will thank yourself in the long run.

Don't end your life full of regrets.
In this story there are no reruns.

So look inside yourself.
Decide what you want to do.

Apply yourself, dig down deep.
And always follow through.

Tell me a story

Cover me with your words.
Let them flow onto my lips.
Every syllable that escapes.
Axhillirates, excites and grips.

Paragraph after paragraph.
Heightening all my senses.
Words roll off your tongue.
As I read my body tenses.
Page after page.
Searching for the Climax.
The reader kept engaged.
There's nothing your style lacks.

Building up my words.
Enough to fill a book.
Stories of bees and birds.
I think i may be hooked.

Burning Heart

There she sat.
In a dimly lit bar.
Drinking her wine.
Mind on the scars.
She left behind.
In a place not far.
Where she reached in my chest.
And tore out my heart.

Reaching into her purse.
She pulled out a light.
Setting it ablaze.
Lighting up the night.

My heart in her hand.
Under neon light.
Fingers wrapped round.
Gripping it tight.

The lit cigarette.
Hung from her lips.
As she raised my heart.
Up to the tip.

No signs of remorse.
Shown on her face.
As she took my heart.
And set it ablaze.

Venomous

Your Venomous tongue has a song to be sung.
On the social ladder you climb another rung.
Spitting your poisonous words all around.
Looking down on your friends who are nowhere to be
found.

Never letting yourself get emotionally attached.
The next victim you seek will soon feel your wrath.

Chewing their hearts up you spit them on the floor.
Have them kneeling before you.
Have them Begging for more.

So pathetic and weak when you listen to them speak.
Pleading in agony, your attention they seek.

You say you've had enough and put your foot down.
A long spiked heel stabbing into the ground.
Your patience is gone now what will you do?
Your needy followers worshipping you.

Monsters

Are there monsters in the dark?
What lurks within the shadows?
Keep your feet tucked in.
Be sure to lock your windows.
Are the demons real?
Or just dancing in your head?
Before you close your eyes.
Always look under the bed.

Anxiety

Thumping in my ear.
THUMP THUMP, THUMP THUMP.
My heart is all I hear.
BUMP BUMP, BUMP BUMP.

Body tensing up.
All my muscles tight.
My bodies way of saying.
"I just don't feel right?"

Can't stop my foot from twitching.
I fidget and squirm in my seat.
I feel like it is winning.
But I just won't claim defeat.

Mind is overactive.
Unfocused but keeps on racing.
Can't ever catch a glimpse of.
Whatever thoughts my mind is chasing.

Deep breathes fill my lungs.
Trying to get it to stop.
But still it continues on.
Wether I want it to or not.

It attacks like a silent killer.
Stalking in the night.
You never see it coming.
Until you've felt it's strike.

Breaths are getting shorter.
My chest is tightening up.
I close my eyes and wish it away.
Please, just make it stop.

Something you can't see.
Can make a grown man weak.
It can fluster your mind so badly.
You find it hard to speak.

We Remember

Let's take a moment and remember the past.

Some silence for the ones who grew up to fast.

Packed up and shipped out.
Shipped off to war.
Bound to their word.
To the oath that they swore.

They stormed the beaches.
And raided the air.
Some soldiers so young.
They should not have been there.

But every loyal soul.

Stood together!!!

Stood strong!!!

They sacrificed their lives.
So yours and mine could go on.

Charging into battle.
Everything on the line.

We must never forget.
The ones who gave their lives.

Sacrificed it all.
Left their family and friends.
Blazing trails on the battle field.
All the way to the end.

So I wear my poppy.
And I wear it with pride.
For all the brave souls.

Who fought...

Who bled...

Who cried...

Shadows

My shadow won't stop following me.
It feels darker and denser today.
No matter how fast I walk or run.
It just won't go away.
The darkness holds my secrets.
Cold fingers grasping tight.
Only when the sun goes down.
Can my shadow avoid the light.

The Mad Poet

A circus of words on the flying trapeze.

Jotting down words with the greatest of ease.

Lyrical genius.
     Accumulating degrees.
          Hands behind your back.
               Now down on your knees.

This is an illegal search and seize.
Kick in your door whenever they please.

Turn us all into.....
Detainees.
Deportees.
Refugees.

We play A rigged game with no referrees.
Always have to agree to keep them appeased.

Every time I write I keep my goals in the scope.
It's a new way I've found to learn how to cope.
Like a tightline walker balancing on a rope.
Help me keep a grip on things or at least that's what I
hope.
Try not to lose my footing it can be a Slippery slope

Words blast off like the man in the cannon.
I'm not scared of the flight, I just hope I stick the
landing.
It's a crazy ride but the view is outstanding.
Sometimes we just need to breeeaaath.
When life gets demanding.

Mind sends a signal and my hand begins to write.
Throwing down words and keeping them tight.
Having revelations like I just saw the light.
Laying it down each and every night.
Read and Reread to make sure it sounds right.
Keep on climbing, reaching new heights.
Always keeping my Goals in sight.
Theres A fire to Ignite.
Im Wound up tight.
A slice of the pie, I want my bite.

Roll into heaven, beat up and disheveled.
To hell with it, I'm just gonna hang with the devil.
Buy me a goat, listen to Heavy metal.
That's what evil looks like if we are being
stereotypical.
Always Hypocritical.
Cunningly Cynical.
Thoughts so subliminal.
Rhyming is mythical.
Becoming more Lyrical.
Situation critical.
A story so biblical.
Since I dropped the umbilical.

AND I'VE YET.....
To reach my pinnacle.

Flow like a river so full of rage.
A rabid animal busting out of its cage.
Open my mouth another verse escapes.
The larger the pot the higher the stakes.
Taking out all of the fakes and the snakes.
Do What it takes.
Those are the breaks.
Body still works even though it aches.
I've definitely made my share of mistakes.
When I stomp my foot the whole earth quakes.

Twisting words up as I spin another story.
Tales of adventure, passion and glory.
I'm never gonna stop So there's no need to worry.
Digging into your mind There's no way to ignore me.
It won't be long until your begging for more of me.

Smoke curling from my pen due to feverish friction.
I can't put it down its like an addiction.
Laying down the law, your in my jurisdiction.
I'm telling you now this shit isn't fiction.

Have you hooked on my words I'm your new guilty
pleasure.
The twists and the thrills are impossible to measure.
With every story I tell I get better and fresher.
Enlightening your mind like a genius professor.

A mad scientist experimenting with words in my lab.
Remove the top of my skull, reach in and I grab.
A handful of words to add to my rant.
I don't want to stop, I won't, I can't.

Like the Wick of a bomb about to blow.
Exploding with words for a dynamite flow.
From the heavens above to the hell below.
All fired up now, cmon, let's go.

A slew of words sewn tightly together.
With a material that's ten times tougher then leather.
Soaring to new heights as I spin my propeller.
Pushing negativity into the cellar.
Rain falls from the sky, much more then a drizzle.
The air around me so hot, I can now hear it sizzle.

Come challenge me and leave on a stretcher.
Your about as hard as a bag full of feathers.
We may have just met but you'll remember me
forever.

Lid rattling on the top of a steaming hot pot.
Dangerously close to boiling over the top.
Once it starts its impossible to stop.
Spilling onto the floor so I go grab a mop.
Bring the pigs to the trough and feed them their slop.
Serving it up while I cut and I chop.
Once I get started I'll be Damned if I'll stop.

Words as dangerous as a double edged sword.
Spit the right ones so they can't be ignored.
A glorious combination when mixed with the right
chords.
Come bow down, kneel to your lord.
I'm speaking the truth this isn't a lore. Smooth like an
eagle that elegantly Soars.
Vicious as the Lion with the fiercest roar.
I can keep it coming if you really want more.
A bottom dweller rising up from the Ocean floor.
Scientists drill into my head, retrieve a sample from
the core.
On the edge of your seat wondering if theres more.
Always going into battle like im on a foreign shore.
I may have came in peace but sir i fear no war.

Unbreakable

My hands are not busy enough.
Can't seem to slow down my mind.
This is the most uncomfortable.
That I've been in quite some time.

Just need to throw down some words.
Something to distract my thoughts.
If this doesn't work then....
I'll try something else perhaps.

Aching badly for someone.
I am craving someone's touch.
Not long before my mind hits overdrive.
Sometimes I'm just too much.

I may not be for everyone.
But all I can be is me.
There are many layers here.
If one truly wants to see.

No idea where im going.
Destination unknown.
An adventure created with pen and paper.
While never Leaving home.

A twister of thoughts.
Tears apart the park.

An exploding tank.
Ignited with a spark.

Blinded by the light.
Come in swinging.

Challenge all my fears.
The bell is ringing.

I'll bring them to tears.
Then walk away singing.

Yes, I can be beat.
It's been done lots before.
But I always get up.
Always ready for more.

You can't keep me down.
You can try all you want.
But I am unbreakable I cannot be stopped.

My heart settles down.
As my mind takes a break.
Soon I will go back.
And look for spelling mistakes.

All of the wrongs.
I made in my haste.
Is it all spelled right?
Properly spaced?

Not sure where it's heading.
Unsure where it will end.
But if I do continue to write.
I'll be needing a new brand new pen.

Why stop writing if the words continue on.
Write yourself a story or poem.
Try to write a song.

Don't let your mind hold you back.
Let it lead you in to battle.
Hit your enemies head on.
Be sure to make heads rattle.

Push yourself.
Challenge yourself.
Take total control.

Love your self.
Take pride in yourself.
To the deepest part of your soul.

I'd love to keep on writing.
But I have run out of time.
My Imaginary adventure is over.
Now back to my real life.

If your still hear with me reading.
Thank you for your time.
I hope you have a fantastic day.
And I hope you've enjoyed my rhymes.

www.ingramcontent.com/pod-product-compliance
Lightning Source LLC
LaVergne TN
LVHW021305200726
843509LV00012B/1790